MONIKA VAICENAVIČIENĖ

WHAT IS A RIVER?

Enchanted Lion Books
NEW YORK

We are on the banks of the river, my grandmother and I.

I am picking flowers. Each flower has a meaning.
Daisies represent love; shamrocks, health; reeds, resilience.
That's what Grandma says. I'm going to make a wreath.

Grandma has a piece of fabric, some thread, and a needle.
She is embroidering a tablecloth.

The river glimmers in the shade, reflecting trees and flowers.
It has hidden depths beneath its surface. Just like people.

"River, who are you?
Grandma, what is a river?"

A RIVER IS A THREAD, says Grandma.

It embroiders our world with beautiful patterns. It connects people and places, past and present. It stitches stories together.

Rivers make up only a tiny fraction of all the fresh water on Earth—just 0.0002%. That's even less than a teaspoon compared to a bathtub! But think of all the powers rivers have: They take us on breathtaking voyages of discovery, soothe with their coolness, bring us together, inspire contemplation, tickle the imagination, and sometimes even frighten us.

- A River Floods -

A RIVER IS A JOURNEY

A bubbling spring, a gap in a glacier, a boggy marsh, a silent lake—a river can begin anywhere.

A river travels to many places: prairies and cities, dense forests and lush meadows, steppes and tundra, mountains and valleys. It travels through heat and cold. It leaps from dizzying heights, cascading down as a waterfall. It slinks lazily through marshes. Suddenly, it twists, then meanders. It creeps underground. It carves canyons out of mountains, reducing rock to sediment. Over time, the sediment accumulates where the river meets the open sea, forming a delta.

Rivers can join together and flow as one, connecting places and people. Can you imagine how many people the Nile— the world's longest river—visits on its 4100-mile journey through Africa? And the Danube in Europe flows through ten countries and gets its water from nine more.

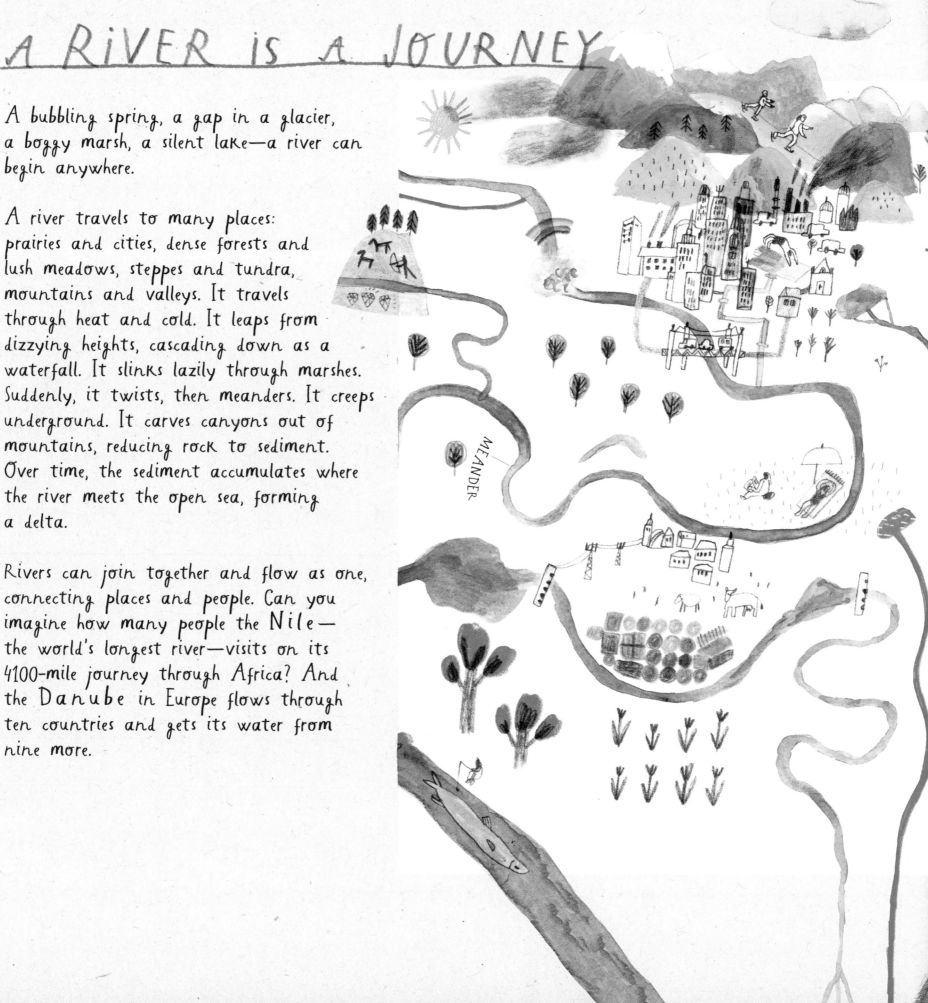

MEANDER

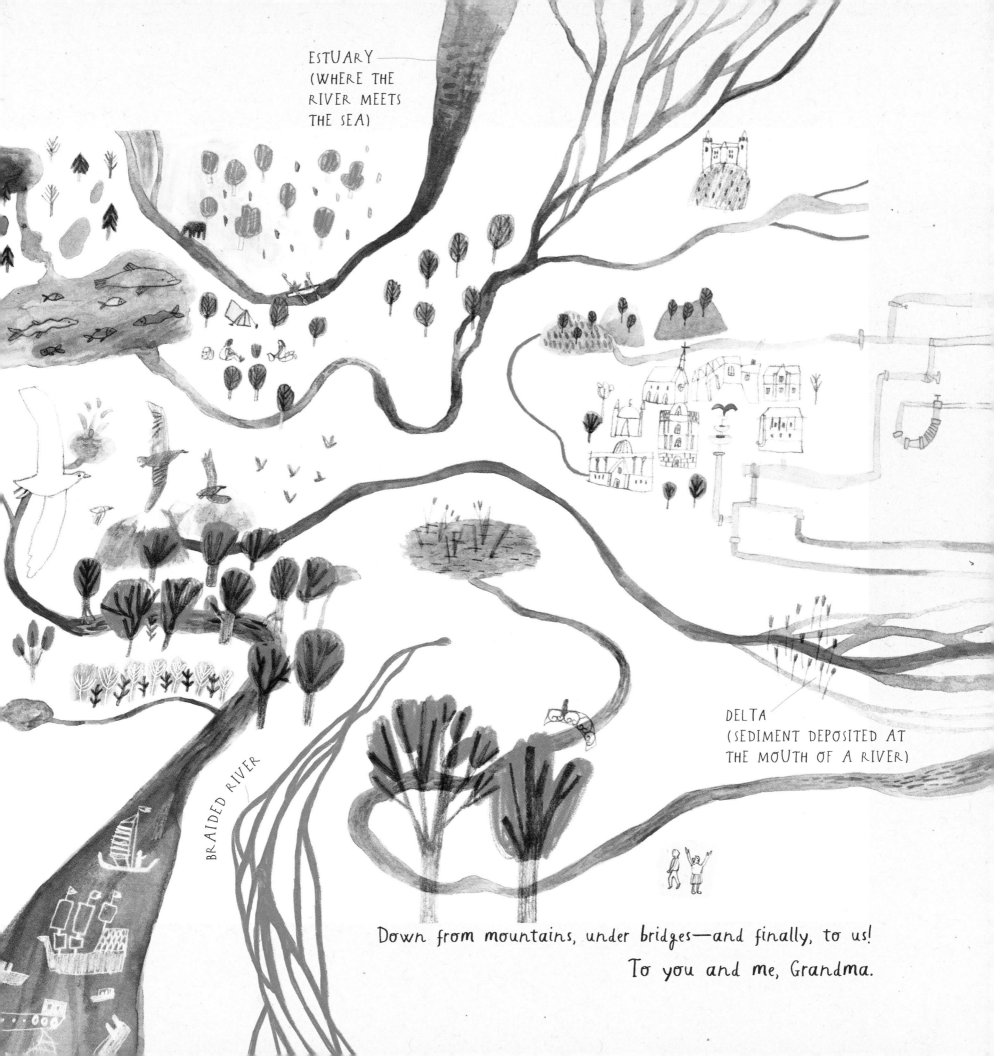

ESTUARY
(WHERE THE
RIVER MEETS
THE SEA)

DELTA
(SEDIMENT DEPOSITED AT
THE MOUTH OF A RIVER)

BRAIDED RIVER

Down from mountains, under bridges—and finally, to us!
To you and me, Grandma.

DRAGONFLY

GIANT SOUTH AMERICAN TURTLE

BEAR CATCHING SALMON

A RIVER IS HOME

Mammals, birds, fish, insects, reptiles—
all kinds of astonishing creatures call rivers
home. Rivers are some of the most diverse
ecosystems on Earth! In fact, they
house more species of fish than the ocean.

People, too, live near rivers, and
have since ancient times. The first
civilizations emerged in the
valleys of the:

Tigris and Euphrates,

Nile,

Indus,

and
Yellow
River,

where their waters had enriched
the land with nutrients and
sculpted natural roads.

CAPYBARA

HIPPOS

PERCH

ARAPAIMA

HERON

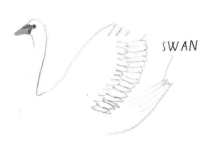 SWAN

 WATER STRIDER

 FRESHWATER PEARL MUSSEL

 KINGFISHER

Rivers create and nourish. They provide drinking water for humans and animals. They i r r i g a t e the fields where we grow food for ourselves and our animals, flowers for our celebrations, and cotton for our clothes.

Rivers make life easier. They provide the water we use to wash our clothes. They produce electricity that powers homes, factories, and mines. They create the sand and gravel we use to construct buildings. We use them to transport goods, whether on huge container ships or small boats.

 PLATYPUS

 IRRAWADDY RIVER DOLPHIN

In recognition of this, many countries have been named after rivers:

BELIZE – THE BELIZE RIVER
BOSNIA – THE BOSNA RIVER
THE REPUBLIC OF THE CONGO
AND THE DEMOCRATIC REPUBLIC
OF THE CONGO – THE CONGO RIVER
GAMBIA – THE GAMBIA RIVER
INDIA – THE INDUS RIVER
JORDAN – THE JORDAN RIVER
MOLDOVA – THE MOLDOVA RIVER
NIGER AND NIGERIA – THE NIGER RIVER
PARAGUAY – THE PARAGUAY RIVER
SENEGAL – THE SENEGAL RIVER
URUGUAY – THE URUGUAY RIVER
ZAMBIA – THE ZAMBEZI RIVER

 AMAZON RIVER DOLPHIN

 MEKONG GIANT CATFISH

RAINBOW TROUT

GIANT OTTER

 HERON

A RIVER is REFRESHMENT

Rivers revive land. Just look at Botswana's inland Okavango Delta. Once a year, the Okavango River floods the plains and creates a wondrous wetland within the Kalahari Desert! Flowers blossom; animals return. All is full of life.

Rivers also refresh us. They bring fog in the morning and birdsong in the evening. They cool our tired feet. With their ceaseless motion, they invite us to see things anew.

HERACLITUS, AN ANCIENT GREEK PHILOSOPHER, WHO SAW THE RIVER AS A METAPHOR FOR CHANGE

For all of these reasons, when a river changes course, the consequences can be dire. Have you heard the sad story of the Aral Sea? Since ancient times, it had been fed by the Amu Darya and Syr Darya rivers. Then, about sixty years ago, people irresponsibly began to divert those rivers to irrigate fields, causing the sea to shrink. Today, the Aral is only a tenth of its former size. Where once there was water, now there are only dusty plains and rusty ships.

BAPTISM IN THE JORDAN RIVER

A RIVER is A NAME

The names of rivers come from different places. Some rivers have names that come from languages so old they no longer exist—languages that were spoken long before any of today's countries were first drawn on maps.

Some rivers have names that describe their movement, like the Tigris ("tiger" in Ancient Greek), Rhine ("that which flows" in Celtic), and Ganges ("swift goer" in Sanskrit).

Some rivers are named after colors, like the Rio Negro with its black waters, the red Colorado River, and the yellow Huang He.

Some rivers have names that describe their size and power— that is how the Mississippi ("big river" in Algonquian), Zambezi ("great river" in Bantu), and Rio Grande ("big river" in Spanish) got their names.

The world's mightiest river is the **Amazon**. Around 20% of all fresh water on Earth flows through it. Every second, it discharges nearly the same amount of water into the sea as all North American and European rivers combined. Its current is so powerful that sailors out at sea can taste its fresh water more than a hundred miles away from the coast!

SPAIN

GREECE

LAND OF AMAZONS

Where does the Amazon's name come from?
Legend tells of an expedition led by Francisco de Orellana during
the ferocious Spanish colonization of South America. While traveling
up the river, de Orellana and his men encountered a band of female
fighters. They reminded him of the Amazons, a tribe of warrior
women whose exploits were described in ancient Greek myth. And so
the river was named. And the story of its name has traveled far beyond
its source, just like its waters.

Some river names are so old that their origins are lost to time, and we
no longer know where they came from. But whether we know the origin
of the name or not, every river's name contains a story—perhaps of
power, love, war, or loss.

A RIVER is A MEETING PLACE

Since the beginning of time, rivers have brought us together through settlement, trade, and ritual. Today, millions of pilgrims gather to wash away their sins and sorrows in the sacred rivers of India, just as they have for hundreds of years.

The Hindu festival of Kumbh Mela, one of the largest peaceful gatherings in the world, takes place on their banks.

THE RIVER GANGES

Areas near rivers are among the world's most densely populated places. China's Pearl River Delta is the largest urban area in the world!

SPIRIT WHOSE NAME YOU HAVE TO GUESS

WHITE HORSE, TEMPTING YOU TO FOLLOW HIM INTO THE FOG

A RIVER IS A MYSTERY

Rivers are full of secrets. What awaits us behind the next bend? That light flickering in the distance—is it a firefly? A campfire? Maybe even a mischievous sprite? What happens on the riverbank at dusk? Who will we find there?

SHAPE-SHIFTING RIVER DOLPHIN CHANGING INTO A MAN AT NIGHT

KING-OF-THE-SALMON,
AS OLD AS TIME

MERMAID,
SINGING SOFTLY

A RIVER is HISTORY

Rivers remind us of the earth's past. They are home to species that originated long before the era of dinosaurs and still thrive today—species called "living fossils." And their currents, which carve canyons from rock, reveal older and older layers.

Rivers also collect fragments of our lives. Sometimes people lose things in rivers, or throw them in on purpose. Some are carried along by the current. Occasionally they resurface; in this way, the river brings us pieces of the past. Others sink slowly down, eventually settling in the mud. Bicycles, keys, mementoes—even memories. People once believed that there was a magical underground river called Lethe. If you drank from its waters, you would lose your memories. But where would they go? Isn't it possible that as people lowered their heads to drink, their memories fell out and sank into the depths? Maybe they are still there, on the river floor, along with the other lost and abandoned things. What we throw away or lose, rivers often hold and remember.

A River is A Smell

Crisp zest of cold water rushing past. Damp scent of mud during low tide. Earthy spice of algae-covered rocks baking in the sun. Sweet perfume of cherry blossom riding on a gentle downstream wind. Irresistible aroma wafting from an open picnic basket by the river. So many smells! But not all of them, as you probably know already, are pleasant!

Imagine the blooming lotus fields
of the Volga River Delta in summer.
Or the floating markets of the
Mekong River. Fresh fruits,
fish, flowers, spices—
everything for sale on the boats
has a smell.

Close your eyes and imagine the river.
What does it smell like to you?
What does it make you think of?

A RIVER is DEPTH

What lies hidden at the bottom of rivers? Stones, plants, abandoned treasures...How many secrets would all the keys thrown into rivers unlock?

What hides in the depths of the Congo,
the world's deepest river?

Over 700 kinds of fish (the river's currents are so strong that different species evolve in different areas, separated by the waters' turbulent flow), crocodiles, tortoises, water snakes, and even mighty underwater waterfalls.

Countless tears swirl there, too, shed long ago, from when a greedy foreign king ruled the river without mercy for its people.

THE CONGO IS OVER 750 FEET DEEP IN SOME PLACES—DEEPER THAN THREE NIAGARA FALLS STACKED ON TOP OF EACH OTHER!

ROI DES BELGES

A RIVER IS ENERGY

Rivers are powerful.
Just think of roaring
waterfalls, or how quickly
rivers can rise and the force
with which they can flood vast
stretches of land.

Once upon a time, Guaira Falls,
on South America's Parana River,
had more water volume than
any other waterfall in the world.
People could hear its roar from
nearly 20 miles away.

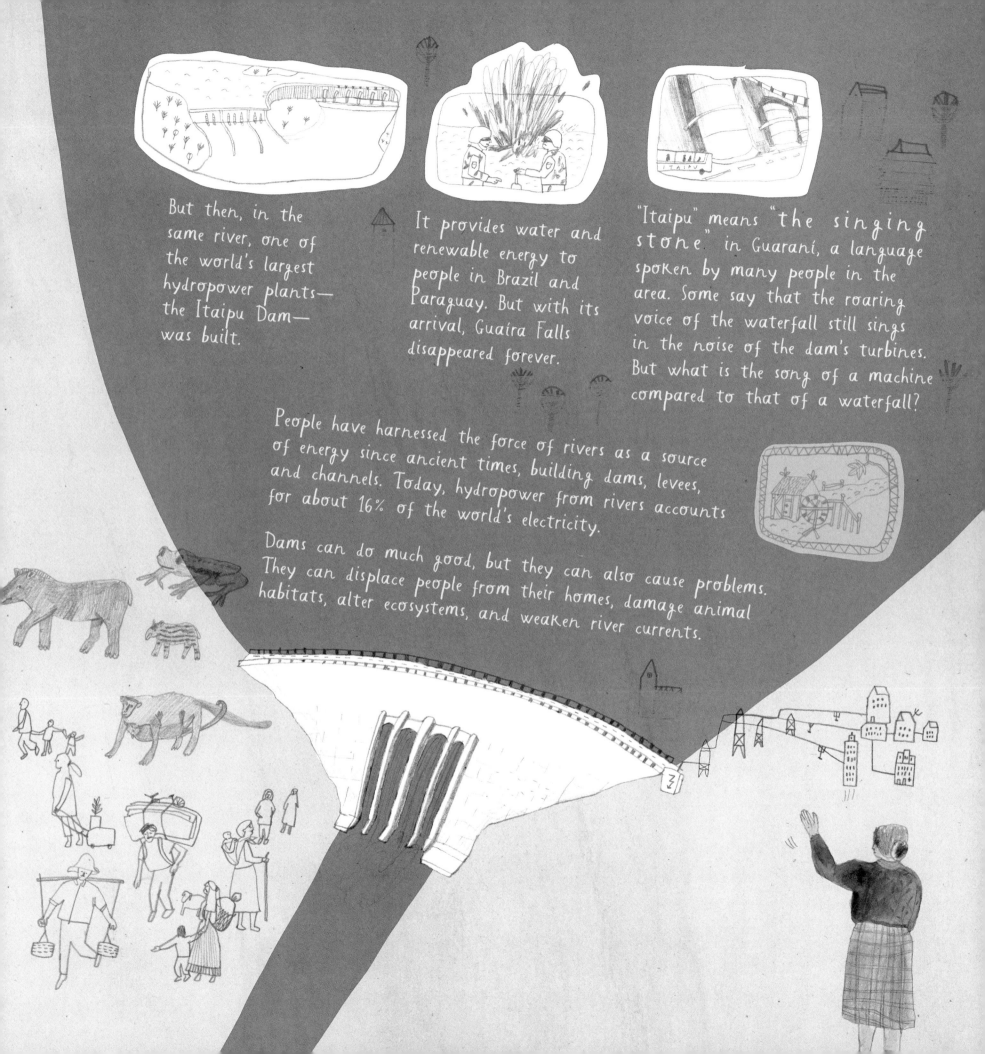

But then, in the same river, one of the world's largest hydropower plants—the Itaipu Dam—was built.

It provides water and renewable energy to people in Brazil and Paraguay. But with its arrival, Guaíra Falls disappeared forever.

"Itaipu" means "the singing stone" in Guarani, a language spoken by many people in the area. Some say that the roaring voice of the waterfall still sings in the noise of the dam's turbines. But what is the song of a machine compared to that of a waterfall?

People have harnessed the force of rivers as a source of energy since ancient times, building dams, levees, and channels. Today, hydropower from rivers accounts for about 16% of the world's electricity.

Dams can do much good, but they can also cause problems. They can displace people from their homes, damage animal habitats, alter ecosystems, and weaken river currents.

A RIVER IS A REFLECTION

Rivers reflect their surroundings, and they tell us about ourselves. So what do they tell us when they are overflowing with garbage and covered in oil spills?

Throughout the ages, people have told stories about a miraculous river that could reverse aging and cure illness. Known as the Fountain of Youth, many have searched for it, such as:

THE GREAT WARRIOR ALEXANDER

FERTILIZERS AND PESTICIDES FROM AGRICULTURE

WASTEWATER CONTAINING TOXIC CHEMICALS FROM FACTORIES

WASTE FROM MINES

SEWAGE RUN-OFF

OIL SPILLS

THE MYSTERIOUS MEDIEVAL KING JOHN (WAS HE AN ACTUAL, REAL PERSON?)

SPANISH CONQUISTADORES

Perhaps such a fountain doesn't actually exist. But like the Fountain of Youth, the flowing water of all rivers is the magical water of life.

CYGNUS,
OR THE SWAN

A RIVER IS A CONNECTION

Rivers connect the past, present, and future. From remote lands, they weave their way to our homes and continue onto distant horizons. They bring faraway places close and turn strangers into neighbors.

Look up on a clear night and you will see a glittering ribbon of stars stretching across the sky. Some call it the Milky Way, some the Path of Birds, and others the Silver River. And like all rivers, it connects us all, for whoever is looking—from wherever they are—shares in its enchantment.

A RIVER is a FLOW

The Ancient Greeks believed that the whole world was encircled by the great river Oceanus, which was the source of all water on Earth. This is where the word "ocean" comes from.

While we now know this isn't the case, it is true that all the water in the world is part of a gigantic system that existed long before we were born and will continue to exist long after we are gone. Water is ever-changing, flowing back and forth between oceans, seas, lakes, rivers, clouds, rain, and groundwater. It flows through every tree, fish, and insect. It flows through you and me.

The sun is sinking in the sky.

Grandma has grown cold. "Time to go home," she says.

"But is the story of the river finished, Grandma?"

She looks at me and smiles.

Painters, composers, sculptors, crafters, explorers, mapmakers, lawmakers, activists, poets, philosophers, pilgrims, conquerors, merchants, fishers, scientists—many people throughout history have told stories about rivers. What is yours?

Every story is important. And new ones are being added all the time. So, you see, the story of the river can never be finished. It is constantly being written.

We are heading home.
But now I know
what my river is:
a story without end.

I finish my wreath
and let the current carry it away.

Thank you
to the geographers:
Dr Nick Middleton, The University of Oxford
Moa Holmlund, The University of Stockholm

for their expertise and time spent reviewing this book

my classmates and the faculty at Konstfack University in Stockholm
for their insightful comments on the early drafts which came into being in 2017

my family

and all those who work diligently to protect our planet

www.enchantedlion.com

First English-language edition published in 2021 by Enchanted Lion Books
248 Creamer Street, Studio 4, Brooklyn, NY 11231
Originally published in Sweden as VAD ÄR EN FLOD?
Copyright © 2019 by Bokförlaget Opal AB, Sweden, 2019
Text and illustrations copyright © 2019 by Monika Vaicenavičienė
English-language text copyright © 2021 by Enchanted Lion Books
All rights reserved under International and Pan-American Copyright Conventions
A CIP is on record with the Library of Congress
ISBN 978-1-59270-279-4
Printed in Italy by Societa Editoriale Grafiche AZ
First Printing